GREAT WREATH IDEAS

GREAT WREATH I·D·E·A·S

TIMOTHY W. FREW

SMITHMARK

A FRIEDMAN GROUP BOOK

This edition published in 1992 by SMITHMARK Publishers Inc.
16 East 32nd Street, New York, NY 10016

ISBN 0-8317-9684-7

GREAT WREATH IDEAS
was prepared and produced by
Michael Friedman Publishing Group, Inc.
15 West 26th Street
New York, NY 10010

Editor: Dana Rosen
Art Director: Jeff Batzli
Designer: Beverly Bergman
Photography Editor: Daniella Jo Nilva

Typeset by Bookworks Plus
Color separations by Excel Graphic Arts Co.
Printed and bound in Hong Kong by Leefung-Asco Printers Ltd.

SMITHMARK Books are available for bulk purchase for sales
promotion and premium use. For details write or call the manager
of special sales, SMITHMARK Publishers Inc., 16 East 32nd Street,
New York, NY 10016; (212) 532-6600.

Acknowledgments

I would like to thank my editor, Dana Rosen, and the designer, Beverly Bergman, for their work on this book of wreaths. Also, craft artist Richard Kollath, who I worked with on my first craft book and who contributed the designs seen on pages 20, 27, 30, 32, 35, 36 (left), 38, 41 (top), 43, 50 (bottom), 51, 56 (top), 57, 58, 60, and 64. I would also like to thank the designers of the other wreaths, including Barbara Radcliffe Rogers, pages 22, 46, 50 (top), 52, and 54; Carol Endler Sterbenz, pages 36 (right), 39, 41 (bottom), and 56 (bottom); and Rob and Lucy Wood, pages 18, 25, 28, 29, 37, 42, 44, 48, 67.

Contents

Chapter One

Wreath Basics

As a response to the increasing rigors of modern society, more and more people are harking back to a time when life was simpler. From rustic interior design and hearty, healthy cooking to rural handicrafts, people are becoming fascinated with all things associated with the country life. Over the past several years, there has been a rebirth in the appreciation of traditional arts and crafts. The simple act of creating, whether it be arranging flowers, stenciling a wall, or making a basket, can be extremely satisfying, especially in our day and age when very few things in our lives are produced by hand.

Along with many other traditional crafts, the art of wreath making is enjoying a renaissance, having progressed far beyond the habitual evergreen wreath hanging on the door at Christmas. In past eras, wreaths were used to celebrate a wide variety of occasions throughout the year. In fact, all through history the shape of the wreath—the circle—has been used to symbolize the changing of the seasons and the different cycles of life.

Once again, wreaths are being displayed at all times of the year, and they are now made from a wide variety of materials—both traditional and nontraditional. From a simple yet beautiful grapevine-and-herb wreath to an elaborate wire wreath incorporating rare and exotic materials, this traditional rural handicraft has developed into an innovative and highly accessible art form.

One of the first considerations when making a wreath is determining what types of materials to use. Dried or fresh flowers, herbs, peppers, gourds, moss, evergreens, cloth, paper—wreaths can be constructed from virtually any material. Materials are chosen for a variety of characteristics. Certain herbs and spices are used purely for the fragrance they emit. Dried or fresh flowers may be used to add color to a design. Ornamental grasses, dried pods, and pine needles may be used simply to add interesting textures to the wreath. When walking through the woods or across fields, always look for interesting materials

that can be used on a decorative wreath. Also, don't limit yourself to the typical: several of the examples in this book were made by using some very unusual objects.

This book is designed to whet the imagination. It is a book of wreath ideas, rather than just a step-by-step instruction manual. The techniques of wreath making are simple and can be learned quickly. The artistic eye needed to conceptualize and execute an effective wreath design, however, can be much more difficult to develop. Examining other people's wreath designs is a great way to develop your own wreath-making ideas. The other way is to simply keep creating wreaths. Keep experimenting, and soon you will be creating wreaths as beautiful as the ones in this book.

Opposite page: Some common wreath bases: a multiwire frame, a braided-rope base, a crinkle-wire frame, a moss base, and a straw base.

BASIC WREATH FORMS

Wreaths can be made from a wide variety of bases—everything from a bent wire clothes hanger to a circular baked loaf of bread. There are, however, four basic types of wreath bases that can be bought premade in craft stores—straw, wire, polystyrene (Styrofoam™), and grapevine. The straw wreath is probably the easiest base to work with. Built by winding straw around a wire base and securing it with nylon string, these bases are durable, easy to handle, and porous.

© Michael Grand

Straw wreaths come in a wide range of sizes and shapes—the two most popular of which are the heart and the basic circle. They are especially popular for use with dried flowers, since the tightly wound straw provides a stable base for the sometimes fragile stems of dried flowers. Because the straw is so dense, however, it is sometimes difficult to push the stems of dried flowers through it. This problem can be solved by wiring the fragile dried materials to florist's picks before inserting them in the wreath base.

The wire base is probably the most widely used frame for the traditional evergreen wreath. Wire bases come in two distinct styles: the crinkle wire frame and the multiwire frame (also called the double-wire frame). The crinkle wire frame is a single piece of heavy wire, bent into a zigzag pattern and formed into a circle. This inexpensive ring is best used for fresh or dried flower arrangements. The zigzag bend in the ring helps hold stems in place. The multiwire frame consists of four wire rings that are wired together to form a three-dimensional base. These sturdy frames are perfect for making fresh garden wreaths, evergreen wreaths, and wreaths made of permanent materials. The double construction of the wire rings provides space for bulky items such as pine cones to be wedged or wired into place.

The polystyrene base is a very easy base to use; however, it is much less durable than the other types of bases, and, therefore, its uses are very limited. There are two different types of foam bases: one is a simple form cut from foam and having flat sides; the other is made from extruded foam. This second type is usually reinforced with a wire ring and is capable of holding heavier weight. If you push too many florist's picks or stems into a polystyrene base, it will break apart. Also, polystyrene limits your design choices. Every inch of the base must be covered so that the white plastic base does not show through; to do this, however, you must use light materials because of the wreath's lack of stability. In addition, polystyrene is not an ecologically sound material.

The final wreath base is probably the most beautiful and the most versatile of all the bases. Grapevine wreaths can be bought in craft stores in a variety of sizes—three inches (7.5cm) to four feet (1.2m)—or they can be easily constructed by hand with loose strands of grapevines. The floral and craft industries have also produced grapevine wreaths in a palette of muted, vivid, and gilded colors that open up a wide range of design possibilities for the wreath maker. A popular variation of the traditional grapevine circle is the grapevine heart. Hearts are a little more difficult to construct by hand; however, they are available in a variety of sizes, thicknesses, and colors at craft stores.

WINDING A WREATH

Winding is a good method to use for adding a covering layer of materials onto a wreath base. This method of adding materials is best used with a wire, polystyrene, or straw wreath base. Most designers wind materials to a wire base because this is the easiest base to work with using this method. Grapevine wreaths are usually too irregular to effectively wind materials to them. Also, winding usually covers the entire wreath base, and grapevines are too visually interesting to completely cover in any wreath design.

When winding a wreath, it is extremely important to have a sturdy working surface. You will also need to have on hand a pair of garden snippers, a spool of waxed twine (waxed twine grips flower and evergreen stems better than unwaxed), and a circular wire base.

Gather together all the materials you wish to wind onto the wreath base. Medium-stemmed flowers and evergreens seem to work best. Make sure you have enough materials for the entire winding job because once you begin, it is not possible to stop and add additional elements. The entire job must be completed at once.

Take a small handful of the flowers or herbs and place them on the wire frame so that the stems run along the wreath base. Hold the frame and the flowers in your left hand and place a length of twine alongside the flower stems. Then wind the spool of twine through and around the wreath in a clockwise direction, making sure all elements are tight and secure. Next make a couple of wraps around the end of the twine to secure it.

Once the first cluster is secure, add another just below it and continue to wind the twine around the base. Continue this process clockwise around the wreath: each time you have secured a handful of flowers to the frame, reapply another cluster of flowers. When you are nearly at the end of the wreath, carefully lift the flower heads of the first cluster and place the stems of the tail-end flowers into place, wind with care, and finally secure the twine with a few good knots. If there are a few spots where the materials are a little thin, simply attach a small cluster of flowers to a florist's pick and insert it into the thin area. The fuller the wound wreath, the better it looks, so don't worry about using too many materials.

© William Seitz (all)

Top and middle: Spanish moss is laid on a straw wreath frame. Florist's wire is inserted into the straw and wrapped around the moss. Bottom: German statice is formed into small fan-shaped bunches and wired onto the straw base.

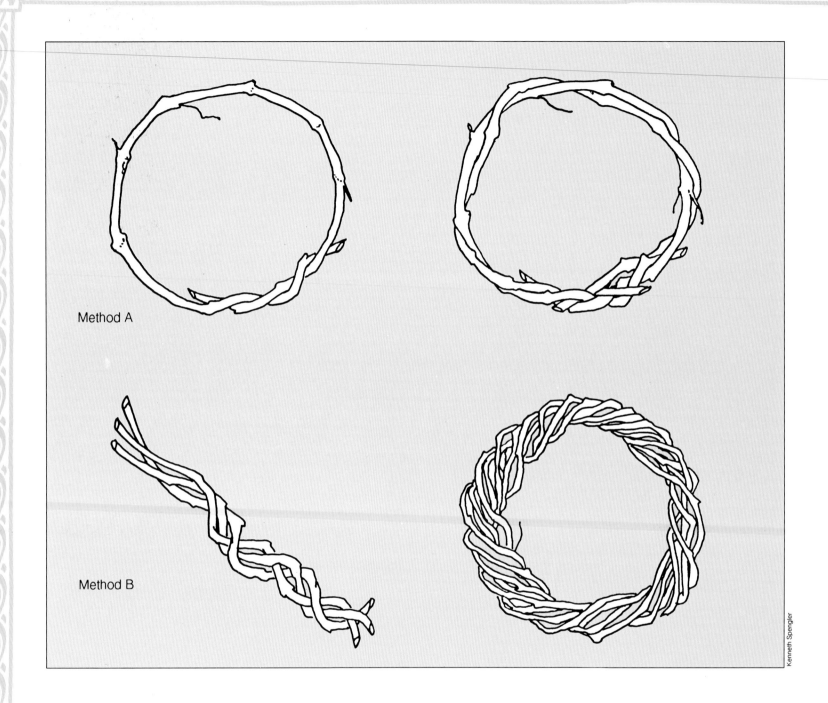

Method A

Method B

Kenneth Spengler

How to Make a Grapevine Base

While grapevine wreaths can be bought premade in virtually any craft or florist store, there is something very rewarding about making your own. Wrapping your own grapevines also gives you more control over the finished look of the wreath. It is very important to pay attention to how tight and how thick you wind the vines when constructing the base, for the degree of firmness and the width will strongly influence the final look of the wreath. Experimentation is the key. The more wreaths you make, the greater control you will have. No matter what size wreath you are attempting, the process is the same, so if you finish a vine base that satisfies your needs but you still have extra vines, take the time to wind another, perhaps smaller wreath. It's always good to have a few extra wreath bases lying around. You never know when you will need a quick party decoration or a gift for a friend.

The process of making a grapevine wreath is really a very simple one that becomes even more so with practice. Loose vines can either be bought at a craft store or collected from the wild. The length of the vine pieces you use will depend upon the size of the base you wish to make.

To make the base, hold the cut end of a vine in your left hand, and with your right hand bend the free end of the vine into a circle, so that you have the approximate size of the final wreath. Clasp the section of the vine where the two ends meet with your left hand: you now have the basic loop that will become the wreath. Now using your right hand, weave the free end of the vine in and out through the loop, securing the two ends by locking them into the vine.

Next, insert one end of your second length of vine into the woven part of the first loop, weave the vine through the wreath, and secure the ends. With each length of vine your wreath will grow in width, so continue this process until you achieve the desired fullness. When ending the wreath, be sure to tuck all loose ends into the body of the wreath.

There is also another method of making a vine wreath. Start by holding three vines in your left hand and then twist them together so that they form a ropelike singular vine. Add additional vines, continuing to twist each one around the wreath so that the final, full wreath is even and dense. Tuck all loose ends into the body of the wreath after you've reached the desired width.

There are definite advantages to making the wreath base very full and asymmetrical rather than clean and even. If the base is irregular and strong, it will be able to hold more objects in unexpected places and therefore give you more freedom in the design. Of course, if you already have a concept for the final wreath design, it will dictate how tight and full you wind the vine base.

After wrapping the wreaths, add a wire loop to the top for hanging. This will give you a reference point for the top of the wreath as well as a safeguard for holding the vines together. Be sure the wire loop is strong and securely attached, for you do not want to lose your creation by it falling off the hook. If you finish your wreath and realize you forgot to add a hanging wire, be very careful not to harm your work when threading the wire through the vine.

There are two ways to make a grapevine base: wrap one length of vine at a time, weaving new lengths around the main body until you reach the desired thickness (top), or begin with three vines twisted together and add more vines one by one until you reach desired width (bottom).

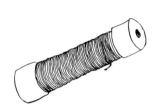

Craft Wire

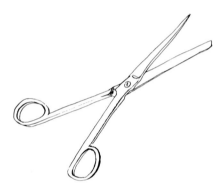

Ribbon Scissors

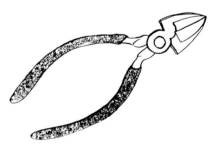

Madeline Sorel

Wire Cutters

BASIC TOOLS

Wreath making is a very simple process that requires few tools and materials. Most of the tools required you probably already have lying around the house. Others can be picked up cheaply at a craft or hardware store. The number and quality of your tools will depend on just how involved you wish to get in wreath making and other types of craft projects. These tools will be very helpful in the construction of wreaths, in the gathering of different materials for further wreath projects, and in any other craft project you may undertake.

Florist Tape

Florist tape works well for repairing damaged stems, disguising wires, and securing materials. While this tape comes in a variety of colors, dark green and dark brown tape are the most versatile, since they effectively blend in with most wreath-making materials. With a little practice, this tape is very easy to use. Place the end of the tape on the end of the wire, stem, or pick at a slight angle. Then, while pulling gently on the tape, spin the wire so that the tape wraps evenly; this will form a tight bond between the tape and the wire. Do not, however, bother to tape wire that will not be visible in the wreath design. Taped florist's wire and long picks make great artificial stems for dried flowers.

Craft Wire

A supply of craft wire, also called florist's wire, is another essential material. This handy wire is available in a variety of diameters and colors. In brown, black, or green, 22- or 24-gauge wire will blend in with most designs and be strong enough to hold even the heaviest of materials. You will need this wire for a variety of purposes: for attaching pods or flowers to wooden picks; for tying bows and other elements to the wreath; and for making a secure loop for hanging the finished wreath. Craft wire is also helpful in reinforcing the brittle stems of dried flowers.

Cutting Utensils

A lot of wreath making involves the cutting and trimming of materials. You will be working with a great deal of wire, wooden picks, paper ribbon, and a wide variety of plant stems. Each of these materials will have to be cut and recut to size as the construction of the wreath takes shape. A well-equipped work area includes a pair of wire cutters, a pair of ribbon scissors, and a pair of garden shears to take care of all cutting needs. Each of these utensils has its own specific purpose, and they can't be doubled up. For example, ribbon scissors are not effective for cutting wire, and garden shears will tear paper ribbon before they cut through it.

While not entirely necessary, a small razor knife, such as an X-Acto™ knife, and a sharp pocket knife are also handy tools to have around. They can be used for more delicate cutting and trimming procedures such as shaving a point on a blunted pick or cutting a design in a paper ribbon.

Very few activities are as enjoyable as going out into the woods and fields and collecting your own wreath materials. A grapevine, a small fir branch, and a few pussy willow stalks all make nice additions to a country wreath. There are a few simple cutting tools that you should take along on any gathering expedition. Again, a good pair of garden clippers, capable of cutting through fairly substantial branches, and a fairly sharp folding pocket knife are essential when gathering materials. A small saw can also be very helpful to have along; some saws are small enough to be fixed within a sheath and attached to a belt, yet are capable of cutting through a small tree or large branch.

Hot-Glue Gun

A hot-glue gun is an inexpensive tool that will greatly enhance your wreath-making capabilities. Sure, you could get by without one; however, I would strongly recommend making the expenditure for this versatile craft tool. Using a dot of fast-drying hot glue is the easiest and quickest way to secure an object to your wreath. Hot-glue guns come in various sizes and price ranges. The small, most inexpensive models operate by thumb pressure and sometimes require two hands to handle properly. The larger trigger-operated models are much easier to use and well worth the few extra dollars you will have to spend. The trigger gun allows more freedom of movement and greater ease in gluing.

If you choose not to purchase a glue gun, you can take care of most of your gluing needs with a bottle or jar of white crafts glue. While this glue does not dry as quickly or hold as well, it will be sufficient in most situations. In fact, even if you do own a glue gun, it is a good idea to have a bottle of this glue on hand for times when a glue gun is inappropriate.

Wooden Florist's Picks

For most types of wreaths (especially dried-flower wreaths), you will need florist's picks for attaching your materials. These picks come in a variety of lengths, three inches (7.5cm), four inches (10cm), and six inches (15cm) being the most common, and they are either green or natural in color. Each pick has a thin wire on top for attaching the flower or other material to it. To attach a flower stem, simply hold the pick and the stem in your hand so that the pick rests on the left side of the stem. Then tightly wrap the loose wire with your right hand. Picks will insert easily into virtually all wreath bases and many other wreath materials. It may be necessary to further secure the pick with a dot of hot glue or some florist's wire.

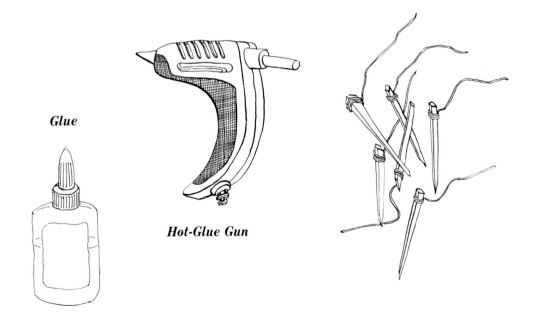

Glue

Hot-Glue Gun

Florist's Picks

HOW TO DRY FLOWERS

Dried flowers are a lovely addition to any wreath. While many varieties of dried flowers are available at garden and craft stores, it is much more satisfying to dry your own flowers that you have picked from your garden or harvested from the wild. Keep in mind that each type of flower has its own particular characteristics, and therefore a particular harvesting time that will yield the best drying results. Cornflowers and bachelor buttons, for example, should be harvested the same day that their buds open and then quickly dried. If harvested at the wrong time, they will be extremely fragile when dried and their color will fade. In contrast, hardy flowers such as celosia and globe amaranth have a picking range of several weeks during their bloom. Through continued gardening and drying of flowers you will gain experience and learn the particular characteristics of each species in your area. Here are a few general rules that will apply to most flowers and will help you to get started:

1. Harvest flowers at or just before their peak blooming period and then quickly dry.
2. Be sure the dew or rain has evaporated from flowers before picking them.
3. Strip off excess (or all, depending on your needs) leaves from the flowers before drying.
4. Harvested flowers should be kept as fresh as possible until they are dried.

There are two basic methods for drying flowers for use in wreath making: air drying and silica-gel drying. Air drying is by far the simplest method. Flowers dried by this method have an imperfect antique look to them and are perfect for certain rustic garland designs. The most common method of air drying is to simply bind bunches of flowers together and hang them upside down in a dark, dry, and warm area such as an attic or a dry tool shed. Any room will do as long as certain requirements such as good air circulation and a minimum of sunlight are met. Certain materials, such as heads of Queen Anne's lace and seed pods, cannot be hung upside down because the petals of the flowers will curl as they close. A better drying method is to place them on a wire screen or on layers of newspapers.

The time needed to dry flowers will depend on the amount of air, heat, and moisture in the room as well as the type of material you are drying. It may range from only a few days to several weeks. Check your flowers from day to day and remove them when the flower petals feel like paper and are no longer soft and pliable. When storing the dried flowers, you should be sure to keep them away from excessive moisture and direct sunlight, as these conditions will shorten the life of the flower.

© Robert Perron

The best way to get beautiful dried flowers is to dry them using silica gel. Silica gel is a sandlike substance that dries flowers within a few days. The gel removes moisture from the flowers, making them usable for wreaths as well as dried flower arrangements and potpourri. Flowers dried by this method retain their original color and structure and in some cases look as though they are fresh instead of dried.

Silica gel can be purchased at most flower or craft stores and is very convenient to use. Although expensive, it can be reused indefinitely. (If it gets moist, heat the gel in an oven set at a low temperature for a few minutes.) Although silica gel is the most efficient medium for drying, sand or a mixture of cornmeal and borax also works. The one disadvantage to using sand or the cornmeal-borax mixture is that it requires a very long period of time. Drying can take anywhere from three to five weeks depending on the type of flower.

The process of drying with silica gel is done in airtight containers to prevent outside moisture from reaching the flowers. First, fill an airtight container about two-thirds full with the gel. Lay each flower in the gel, petals up. Next, pour gel around and over the flowers until they are completely covered, being careful not to damage the blooms. Seal the container and in three days check the progress. In most cases three or four days is suffic-

ient, but heavy-stemmed, thick-petaled flowers may require up to two weeks to dry completely.

Removing the dried flowers is perhaps the trickiest part of the process, because they have now become very fragile and can easily break apart. The best method is to place a slotted spoon under the petals and gently lift the flower out. After removing the flowers, store them in another plastic box with a quarter-inch (6mm) of gel covering the bottom in order to preserve their dryness until you are ready to use them.

Drying flowers allows you to keep out-of-season flowers for use year-round, thereby expanding your wreath-making palette in every season. The silica-gel process works not only with home-grown flowers but with store-bought flowers as well. The key element to remember is that the flowers should be in perfect condition, and they should be dry and fresh when placed in the gel. The fresher the flower, the more successful the result. If a few petals fall off of your dried flowers as you remove them from the silica gel, simply reattach them with a dot of white glue.

© Christopher Bain

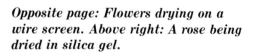

Opposite page: Flowers drying on a wire screen. Above right: A rose being dried in silica gel.

Chapter Two

Wreaths
with
Dried Flowers,
Herbs, *and* *Grasses*

Dried flowers, herbs, and wild and ornamental grasses make extremely versatile and lovely wreath materials, for the variety of colors, textures, shapes, and scents that these materials provide is almost endless. Even many plants that are normally considered "weeds" can make stunning additions to wreaths and dried-flower arrangements. You should keep an open mind when choosing your materials. Always look for the unexpected and use it in a creative way. The designs included in this chapter range from the everyday to the truly unique; you can use these wreaths as a springboard for your own ideas.

This medieval dried-flower-and-herb wreath was inspired by a page out of history. The medieval cloisters were known for their impeccably designed herb and flower gardens; during the Middle Ages, much was learned about the culinary and medical uses of herbs and plants. This elegant herb-and-flower wreath, shown here hanging on a colonial door at the Ladew Topiary Gardens in Monkton, Maryland, makes use of a careful rhythm of colors, textures, and shapes to evoke a feeling of ancient times. The designers were careful to choose only herbs and flowers that were known to have been grown in medieval gardens.

In making this wreath, the wire base was first covered with a background of soft ambrosia. The designers then experimented to find what they considered the correct positioning for the rest of the elements, including nigella, bay leaf, wild marjoram, different colors of larkspur, yellow and white yarrow, boxwood, rosemary, sage, tansy, and Queen Anne's lace. Often the finest wreaths are not entirely planned out before they are made. Rather, they are created during the construction process.

Opposite page: Hanging on a rustic door at Ladew Topiary Gardens in Monkton, Maryland, this wreath was constructed on an ambrosia-covered base with an assortment of herbs and flowers that were commonly grown in medieval cloister gardens.

Dried flowers, or everlastings, are perhaps the most rewarding materials to work with when constructing a wreath design—particularly when you grow, pick, and dry your own flowers. By using silica gel, the flowers retain their brilliant natural hues and varied textures after being dried, and with proper care they can last for years.

This wire-based wreath utilizes beautiful dried flowers, which are placed sparsely in the design. However, the wreath has a lush, sensuous feel to it because the entire wire base was first covered in moss. Moss is very easy to apply to a wire base, and it can be used in many lovely wreath designs. All you need to do is apply hot glue to the sheet moss and carefully fold it around and over the wire frame, making sure that it covers snugly. The amount of moss you use depends on the size of the wreath and the degree of fullness you wish to achieve. Wait until the glue is dry and the moss is completely secure before adding the other elements to the wreath.

This design makes use of silica-dried roses, rose hips, and dusty miller. Rose hips can be harvested from the wild during autumn or they can be bought at the florist shop. When drying roses, allow them to open before putting them in the silica gel, but be sure that they are still fresh. It is best to place the roses in the gel as soon as

© Christopher Bain

they have opened to the degree you desire. Dusty miller leaves can be effectively air dried on a wire screen. For this wreath, however, the designer simply put them in the silica gel along with the roses.

Opposite page: Moss-and-dried-flower wreath on a wire base. Above: These dried flowers are the designer's palette; the bright pinks and reds can be mixed with baby's breath to create rich, eye-catching patterns.

© William Seitz

Wild grasses and sedges are often overlooked as materials for wreath designs. Yet they, too, can be effectively used either as a single element in a dried-flower arrangement, or as the sole dominant motif in a country wreath, as with the wreath on the left. While dried wild and ornamental grasses do not add a great deal of color to a wreath, they do contribute swirls of subdued texture and an overall sense of movement. Very few plants evoke the mood of the autumn harvest better than the flowering heads of wheat, fountain grass, and blue fescue. When dried, grasses take on gold and straw colorations that can be just as interesting as the most colorful flowers. Grasses can be dried and then wound to a wire base. Grass wreaths can also be made fresh and the grasses allowed to dry while on the wreath.

The base of this wreath is constructed of several strands of raffia wrapped around a double-wire wreath frame. This simple grain circle, a symbol of plentiful harvest, is made by laying the bundles of grain along the frame and wrapping them with wire. Additional bundles are attached in a clockwise pattern so as to entirely cover the wire.

Opposite page: This grain wreath on a wire base has long been considered a symbol of a plentiful harvest. Right: The circle-of-grain wreath, or any similar design, is best chosen by someone with a field of grain at his or her disposal.

© Nancy Hill

This wreath adds a soft autumnal touch to any home.

The design below uses a variety of dried flowers to form a lush, full wreath with rich textures and pastel colors. The wreath was made using the winding method described on page 11. Winding a wreath with several different materials is a little more com-plicated than winding with just one. Because it is more difficult to get a feel for how the finished design will look, you must be very careful about the placement of the materials. The best method is to use small bunches of materials and alternate contrasting

© Anita Sabarese

colors, textures, and shapes in order to provide an effective rhythm and balance to the design.

A good place to start when choosing flowers for a particular design is to first think how and where the wreath is to be used. Is it a gift to express love for a friend, a centerpiece for a holiday table, a permanent decoration on a formal mantelpiece? Quite often the function of the wreath helps determine what materials will be chosen. Certain flowers are traditionally associated with certain events. For example, the wedding wreath on this page makes use of flowers that have symbolic meanings. The designers chose rosemary, which symbolizes remembrance and faithfulness; sage, which symbolizes health and long life; white flowers, such as the lily, which symbolize purity; and myrtle, which symbolizes love.

This wreath was designed to be used as a chaplet crown for the bride. The design makes use of a Spanish-moss-covered wire ring adorned with a variety of pastel dried flowers and herbs. Among the whites are Queen Anne's lace, white narcissus, ammobium blossoms, white globe amaranth, and bells of Ireland. The gentle colors come from pink globe amaranth, pink larkspur, nigella pods, yellow statice, and pink strawflowers.

This wreath of dried flowers and herbs was originally designed as a chaplet crown.

© William Seitz

One of the most important charac-teristics of a dried- or fresh-flower wreath, which cannot be adequately conveyed in this book, is aroma. Dried-flower wreaths can be used as a fra-grant potpourri to sweeten the smell of any room. Nothing evokes a mem-ory or sets a mood quite like fra-grance. Air drying certain flowers is a powerful way to preserve the smells of a certain season. Why would you want to use a chemical-filled air freshener when a lovely wreath can work around the clock to freshen a room? The wreath on this page makes use of ex-tremely fragrant and beautiful flowers and herbs to create a circular pot-pourri for the wall.

To create your own wreath pot-pourri, use aromatic flowers such as roses, lavender, chamomile, orange blossom, marigold, jasmine, lime flowers, and scented geraniums, as well as herbs such as mint, lemon balm, lemon verbena, tansy, berga-mot, and sweetfern. Wreaths can also make use of such flowers as strawflow-ers, statice, delphinium, celosia, wild grasses, marigolds, zinnias, and calen-dula more for color and bulk than for pure fragrance. In creating a pot-pourri, it is best to air dry flowers instead of silica drying them. Tie the flowers into bundles and hang them upside down in an airy, shady place. Hanging them inside a paper bag is an effective way to keep them clean and prevent the loss of little pieces. An-other method is to lay them flat on a wire screen or a layer of newspaper, again in a dry, shady place.

The designer of the wreath on page 27 used a green background, in this case sheet moss covering a straw heart base, to create a very simple yet beautifully rustic dried-flower wreath. The wreath maker simply glued the sheet moss down with a glue gun and then attached clusters of silica-dried

© Robert Perron

© Robert Hoebermann

pansies and Johnny-jump-ups to the base. As with the medieval wreath (see page 18), the designer here used a system of intuition and trial and error in arranging the dried flowers on this wreath. And although the elements are far fewer in variety and number, he was able to use size variations and color changes in order to develop an interesting rhythm to the design.

Opposite page: This everlastings wreath contrasts wild grasses with bright red and pink strawflowers. Above: Heart-shaped wreath of moss and sparsely placed dried flowers.

Thomas Jefferson was a man who held great reverence for beauty and practicality. One of the United States' founding fathers and an admired president and statesman, Jefferson was also an avid gardener and lover of agricultural beauty. Monticello, his beloved home in Charlottesville, Virginia, contained countless ornamental gardens as well as extensive terraced vegetable beds. When Jefferson was an ambassador to France, he brought back plants and landscaping ideas for what he called his *Ferme Ornée* (ornamental farm).

It is in the Jeffersonian spirit that the designers put together this exquisite garden wreath seen on this page. With the great statesman in mind, they gathered a collection of flowers, grains, and beans known to have been grown by Jefferson at Monticello. Included here are oriental poppy pods, globe thistle, nigella, dusty miller, bergamot, yarrow, larkspur, button mums, plume celosia, and blue salvia from Monticello's walk; oats, corn, and wheat from the fields; hot peppers, chive flowers, and a single dried chick pea from the vegetable terraces; and

sweet gum balls, pinecones, milkweed pods, wildflowers such as Queen Anne's lace, and wild yarrow as some samples of wild materials available in Virginia during Jefferson's time. All in all there are more than twenty different plant elements working in this colorful wreath, all hot-glued to a moss-covered wire base. It is a stunning tribute to the man and a clever wreath with a theme.

The old adage, "An apple a day keeps the doctor away" comes to striking fruition in the theme wreath on page 29, a unique get-well wreath constructed on a base of dried apple slices. To construct the base, the wreath makers sliced apples to a thickness of about one-eighth inch (3mm) and dried them in an oven. They hot-glued the slices to a thin cardboard ring, allowing the slices to hang over the edge. They then added a variety of traditional healing herbs such as sage, rosemary, tansy, feverfew, and rose hips. For additional color and texture, the designers added silica-dried hydrangea, globe amaranths, larkspur, caspia, roses, love-in-a-mist, and strawflowers.

© William Seitz

Left: A Jefferson-inspired garden wreath. Opposite page: This get-well wreath with dried-apple base has a number of traditional healing herbs, as well as several other herbs added for color.

Wire bases are best used in wreath designs that are full and flowing. They are extremely strong and durable bases and can hold large amounts of heavy materials. Virtually anything can be easily attached to a wire base either by wiring, hot-gluing, or winding on. The design on page 30 makes use of a wire base to create a full rose-hip wreath. This wreath was constructed using the winding technique (see page 11). Simply gather the rose hip clusters in small bunches, lay them against the wreath base, and wind twine around to secure. This single-element design is perfect for a wire base. The rose hips were put on full and thick, not allowing any of the base to show through. If you want a design that reveals some of the base, choose a grapevine or a straw base.

Dried herbs add texture and aroma to any wreath design. They can be added in small clusters to accent a floral wreath, or they can be used as a dominant element in a design. Many people enjoy constructing dried-herb wreaths for the kitchen because portions of the wreath can be used in cooking and then replenished as the wreath becomes too bare.

The herbs on the country wreath pictured on this page were added using the winding method (see page 11). Small violet flowers were also added to the design for a touch of color.

Herbs can either be added fresh and allowed to dry on a wreath, or they can be dried beforehand. The best method for drying herbs is by air dry-

© Lynn Karlin

ing. Never dry herbs using silica gel if you plan to cook with them. Harvest the herbs before the plant blooms; late morning, after the dew dries but before the midday sun hits, is the best time. Cut the entire stem of the herbs, tie them by the bases of the stems in bunches, and hang them upside down in a dry, dark room.

Opposite page: Rose-hip wreath constructed by winding the clusters onto a wire base. (Be careful of the thorns.)
Above: Herbs and small violet flowers are wound onto a wire base, resulting in this dark wreath mixed with subtle colors.

Chapter Three

Grapevine Wreaths

The grapevine base is one of the most charming and versatile of all wreath bases. It can be tightly wrapped for a dense, full look or loosely entwined for a more rustic appeal. These bases are easy to make from raw grapevines (see page 12), or they can be bought pre-wound at virtually any craft store in a variety of sizes and shapes—including the ever-popular heart wreath.

A lot of the charm of a grapevine-wreath design comes from the base material itself. The grapevine holds a natural, bucolic beauty that provokes thoughts of windswept autumn fields. When creating a grapevine wreath, it is best to keep things simple. Choose only a few elements that complement and harmonize with the organic charm of the woody vine and allow large sec-

tions of the base to show through. If your desire is to create a full, lush wreath with a large variety of decorative elements, then it is probably best to choose another type of base.

This wreath with a premade heart base provides a great example of a sparse yet effective wreath design. The designer used a single type of flower, in this case silica-gel dried wild roses, and allowed much of the vine base to show through.

The most important element in this wreath is the balance between the sparse, delicate roses and the heart shape. Rose clusters were wired around the sides of the heart, eventually coming together at the top of the heart shape. The rose leaves were included to help fill out the heart shape,

while providing a support for the rose clusters and a nice color contrast.

The designer purposely chose small rose clusters in order to keep the decorative elements of the design in scale with the size and thickness of the base. Scale is an important factor to keep in mind when making a wreath. Elements that are too large will dominate, thus creating a heavy, awkward look. But if they're too small, they tend to get lost and the design will lack visual interest. This heart wreath is simple, yet very appealing.

Opposite page: Dried red roses and rose leaves on a heart-shaped grapevine base.

Loose grapevines can be either bought or clipped from the wild. Many designers find that a greater degree of satisfaction comes from going on a hike through the woods or fields and gathering their own vine material. These vines also tend to have more character and earthiness than those found in craft stores, which can sometimes look too perfect. The size and thickness of the vine sometimes do as much to define the visual effect of the wreath as the elements that are added to it.

In the wreath pictured on these pages, the designer used thick vines that he gathered himself. It is the size and shape of these vines that helped to determine the completed form of the design. In addition, open spaces within the structure of the wreath allow the vine itself to become a dominant element. Note that the designer deliberately did not aim for symmetry or equal fullness throughout, thus further enhancing the wreath's rusticity and natural charm.

The vines used in this wreath included natural clusters of fresh grapes and grape leaves. These clusters were actually part of the vine itself and were not added later. As the grapes and the leaves dried, they became very brittle, adding to the rustic look of this wreath. The open segments of the loosely wound vines provided the perfect anchors for clusters of yarrow, cockscomb, and stems of flat-leaf eucalyptus. Small branches of fresh bay-

© Derek Fell

berry were also added as contrast to the deeper tones of the yarrow and cockscomb.

Opposite page: Rustic wreath of dried flowers and bayberry on a grapevine base, which was loosely wound to achieve a natural look. Above: Cultivated grapevines growing along a wire fence. Right: The same rustic wreath, here pictured in its entirety.

© Robert Hoebermann

The lovely springtime wreath pictured directly below makes use of a full, twisting vine base with loose flowing tendrils in the traditional circular shape. The elements in this wreath are all fresh instead of dried. Fresh flowers attached to a wreath will do very well for a limited period of time if they are first placed in water tubes, which are available through your florist. A fresh-flower wreath placed on the front door makes a wonderful welcome sign for a spring party as well as a colorful centerpiece for the dinner table. With just a few fresh flowers you will have a beautiful decorative piece that can last for up to a week if kept watered. And even after the flowers dry, other elements can be added for a whole new design.

Ammobium flowers, hydrangea florets, pink globe amaranths, asparagus fern, and Queen Anne's lace all combine to lend an intensely romantic air to the Victorian heart wreath on page 37. All of the elements on this wreath were dried with silica gel in order to retain their naturally subdued coloring. The wreath base alone evokes an underlying sensuality and romance with its twisted vines and extravagant, curly tendrils. The central focus of the wreath is the bouquet of pink globe amaranths, asparagus fern, and Queen Anne's lace placed on the bow of the wreath. These were actually the final elements to be hot-glued to the heart-shaped wreath base.

Left: Fresh-flower wreath on a grapevine base. Below: This wreath was made by first twisting one stem of silk sweet peas into a loop, then twining two more stems around it. The flowers were then arranged as desired and the wreath was placed on the cherub's hands. Opposite page: Victorian heart wreath.

The commercially bleached wreath on page 38 provides a great base for the warm beige tones of dried pods, ferns, yellow roses, and bleached pine cones. The elaborate cornhusk bow at the top of the wreath nicely balances the clustered elements at the bottom, providing a very tight, tailored look. This bow was constructed with small clusters of cornhusk loops, which were wired onto short florist's picks and inserted directly into the wreath structure. A hot-glue gun was then used to secure the clusters in place. By using these small clusters of cornhusk, you have the ability to make the bow as generous or as sparse as you like. The cornhusk cluster on this wreath was made just large enough to mirror the similar cluster of yellow roses and pods at the bottom, which were glued onto the wreath base.

The wreath on the right began with a 10-inch (25cm) peeled willow base—a simple and elegant wreath by itself. To form the berry swag, a stem of red berries and a stem of black berries were intertwined and bent into a "C." The swag was placed on the bottom front of the wreath, its stems tucked into, and leaves threaded through, the willow vines and then attached with hot glue. The ribbon, tied in a bow and attached to the center of the swag, was the final touch.

Opposite page: Bleached wreath with cornhusks, dried pods, ferns, yellow roses, and bleached cones. Right: Willow wreath with berry swag.

© Jennifer Levy

Interesting textures, fragrant scents, and subtle coloring combine to create a rustic charm on the herb-and-flower grapevine wreath pictured below. The thyme, oregano, and lavender add interesting textures and scents, contrasting nicely with the yellow of the wispy cornhusks and the dried safflowers. The tightly wound grape-vine base provides a sturdy frame-work in which to insert the decorative elements. When using plants that are small and thin, such as these herbs, it is important to choose a wreath base that is tightly woven and has only small spaces between the individual vines. This makes attaching the thin elements much easier and produces a fuller look to the wreath. The amount of flowers, herbs, and other dried materials you attach will vary, depending on the size of the wreath and the effect you hope to achieve.

The wreath maker added materials to this wreath a little at a time to three basic areas: the upper right side; just to the right of the bottom center; and the lower left side. As a result, the wreath is half filled in a semicircle, leaving a large expanse of vine showing. The focal point of the wreath is the creamy safflower cluster on the right-hand side. The placement of the cluster just off center makes the design much more visually interesting than if it had been purely symmetrical. The sprays of dried material that extend upward on the right side and downward on the left seem to radiate from the safflowers, creating a sense of movement in the design. The herbs used on this wreath were added fresh and allowed to dry after the wreath was completed. Fresh herbs are much easier to work with than dried herbs, which tend to be very brittle.

The wreath in the upper right-hand corner of page 41 provides a vibrant celebration of the fall season. Baby pumpkins, gourds, bittersweet, straw-flowers, and sunflowers, together with the vibrant colors of cockscombs, Japanese lanterns, and vivid purple statice, all placed on a burgundy grapevine wreath, make this wreath explode with color. Vine wreaths can either be dyed by hand or bought pre-

© Tony Cenicola

dyed in a spectacular array of colors and tonal values. Vine colors can be used to enhance or complement the added materials of the composition, as this burgundy base sets off the brilliance of these autumn elements.

Many of the materials used in this wreath are perishable and will eventually have to be replaced. You should look at this constant state of change as an advantage. As you add and replace certain elements, the wreath will take on a whole new look and personality. And some of the fresh elements will dry while on the wreath, becoming permanent fixtures.

Even in a full wreath such as this, some of the vine is allowed to show through. Certain elements, such as the bittersweet, burst from the contour of the wreath form, echoing the way it grows in the wild. Overall, the composition is heavy, but balanced and extremely interesting. While this wreath is shown hanging on a mantlepiece here, it can also be laid flat with candles placed in its center to provide a colorful centerpiece to an inviting Thanksgiving supper.

The wreath in the lower right-hand corner of this page was constructed on a teal-colored vine base, providing a beautiful contrast with the other elements used. Hybrid tea roses were hot-glued to the top, golden yarrow and green angel's lace were added in a spray pattern, and rosebuds were then hot-glued onto either side in a narrow line to create a swaglike look.

Lastly, a collar of rose leaves was glued around the design and a long, flowing bow was attached to the top.

Opposite page: Herb-and-flower wreath on a tightly wound grapevine base. Above: Autumnal wreath on a burgundy grapevine base. Right: Teal-colored vine wreath with rose swag.

While hiking through the woods or open fields, or while taking a vacation to another part of the country, a creative wreath maker always keeps an eye out for new and unusual wreath-making materials. Exotic flowers, dried pods, leaves, and berries abound on forest floors. While these natural treasures make some of the most rewarding wreath materials, many exotic flowers, pods, and plants collected from all over the world are available through your local florist and craft stores and can add much to your wreath designs.

The two wreaths on these pages are very similar in design and overall execution, yet the one on the left was constructed entirely from materials the designer found in the woods. The wreath on the right was constructed primarily from store-bought materials. Both wreaths make use of very spare, thin vine bases, made from only two or three wraps of the grapevine. This allows for a very linear, simple look and is quite different from the floral lushness that many people associate with wreaths.

The wreath on the left was made from several strands of richly tendriled wild grapevine found on the edge of the woods. The designers gently formed the grapevine into a circle, allowing many of the tendrils to flow free. They then wired on cranberries, nuts, and holly. This particular wreath is several years old. When it was first made the berries were fresh, but in time, they dried and wrinkled. The

© Robert Hoebermann

designers later decided to refurbish the wreath, while still maintaining the look of the original. Therefore, they kept all of the originally attached elements, including the holly, which had dried to a creamy brown; then rose hips, bean pods, and okra pods were either glued onto the wreath or entwined in the grapevines.

In the wreath above, the designer wrapped a few lengths of bleached vines around a natural vine wreath to create the base. Clusters of sea-grape leaves and an array of bleached and preserved pods, in addition to chico, okra, curly protaea, flat canella, and sponge mushrooms all combine to give this wreath an interesting mix of textures and warm beige colors.

Opposite page: Wreath of dried pods, rose hips, vine tendrils, and holly leaves. Above: Grapevine wreath with bleached vines, sea-grape leaves, and an array of bleached and preserved pods.

In contrast to the two spare, linear wreaths on the previous pages are these three densely wound grapevine designs. The wreath on the left makes extensive use of materials native to Scotland. The focal point of this large wreath is an authentic Scottish brooch, from which sprays of purple heather seem to radiate in all directions. This brooch-heather cluster is actually a wreath unto itself, which was previously constructed and then hot-glued to the final design.

Scotch broom, wild roses, and hawthorn spray out beneath the Scottish brooch-heather cluster. In addition, a delicate vine of white-blossomed heather was attached to the right side

of the wreath, making it look as though it was growing up the side of the wreath. The entire decorative cluster on the bottom of the wreath reaches nearly four feet (1.2m) in width, yet it remains in scale with the large, thick grapevine base and the rustic baronial fireplace upon which it has been placed.

But not all large wreath bases require elaborate decorative elements. The wreath in the lower left-hand corner of this page makes use of an equally bulky and thick vine base. This base, however, was constructed by winding the vines in a spiral pattern, as opposed to the purely circular construction of the Scottish wreath. The spiraling vines serve as a perfect backdrop for the simple clusters of red berries and their yellow leaves. In time, these berries will dry and darken and the wreath will take on a whole new look, providing a good base for a new wreath design.

The wreath on the right achieves a more original look by "escaping" the confines of its circular structure. On a base of pale grapevines, the designers wired an exuberant topping of red everlastings in a sunburst pattern. The deep green sprigs of ivy, inserted along the top curve of the pale vines, provide a beautiful contrast to the deep red tones. This Christmas wreath stands apart from the rest not

only because of its design, but also due to the incorporation of such elements as cockscomb, spike, and sumac rather than the usual types of evergreens. Simple in design and very easy to construct, this wreath was originally designed for Christmas but can be hung and enjoyed year-round.

Opposite page: Wreath with Scottish brooch and purple heather attached to a larger grapevine base. Left: Wreath of red berries and yellow leaves on grapevines wound in a spiral. Above: Grapevine-based wreath with red everlastings.

Chapter Four

Cornhusk
and
Raffia Wreaths

Cornhusks and raffia are extremely attractive and versatile materials to work with in wreath making. They can be added in short, cropped bows or ties to make a wreath with geometric intricacy and interesting texture, or used as long, flowing tendrils to add movement to a design. Cornhusks, popular in the folk arts, are often used in harvest wreaths because they evoke the feeling of autumn. Raffia, a material made from palm, is another favorite of craftspeople, for it is strong, flexible, and attractive.

Cornhusk and raffia are excellent ways to add a country or earthy flavor to a design. They combine well with herbs, dried peppers, seed pods, and a variety of other materials—even an animal skull—to make extremely interesting wreaths.

This fringed cornhusk wreath was constructed by attaching a series of cornhusk bows to a single wire frame. When working with dried cornhusks, it is best to soak the husks in water for about ten minutes to soften them before you begin working. Dried cornhusks are very fragile and may break apart when tied and handled.

For this wreath, the designer knotted one-inch-wide (2.5cm) and six-inch-long (15cm) cornhusks to the wire ring, butting the knots flush up against each other. To knot them, the husks were folded in half lengthwise and the two folded ends were brought over the wire and through the loop and then pulled tight. She then trimmed the ends of the husks to make an even circular form. Next, the designer weaved a brown ribbon around the base of the cornhusk knots. Yellow flowers were added to the design at the end as an embellishment.

Opposite page: Fringed wreath constructed of cornhusk bows.

This Southwestern wreath featuring Indian corn and a bleached animal skull was inspired by the paintings of Georgia O'Keeffe, one of the designers' favorite artists. According to the designers, "Her vision evokes many mysteries, whether the inner sensuality of flowers, the arid grandeur of Southwestern landscapes, or the monumental dignity of bleached bones."

The base of this wreath was formed by connecting three ears of Indian corn, all pointing downward, with their husks pointing toward the sky; extra husks were also added to give it a bit more fullness. Next, sprays of wheat, foxtail grass, sorphum, lone pinecones, honey locust pods, okra pods, fern leaves, and sea oats were all added, in such a way that they seem to radiate from the center of the design.

The crowning touch to this wreath is the prominent animal skull at the center of the design. The designers found this skull, possibly of a raccoon, while on a hike. Still, even after the wreath was seemingly finished, the designers were not entirely satisfied and were bothered by what they considered an inadequate variety of tones. The solution to their tonal problem was the addition of five dried chili peppers. These peppers, a virtual symbol of the Southwest, helped to enhance the rich, warm brown-red tones of the corn and made the wreath complete.

Opposite page: Ears of Indian corn and a bleached animal skull in a wreath inspired by the paintings of Georgia O'Keeffe. Right: Indian corn.

© Derek Fell

Like the O'Keeffe-inspired wreath (see page 48), Indian corn features prominently in the large straw-based harvest wreath pictured below. Here, the designer twisted long lengths of raffia together and wrapped them loosely around the lower portion of a straw ring, adding texture and interest to the base. He then added corn and dried chili peppers to the top of the wreath to enhance the Southwest flavor of the design. The small ears of corn, attached by wiring them onto florist's picks and inserting them into the wreath, seem to cascade from the top of the wreath, like whole ears falling off the harvester's wagon. The husks were gathered into a great tuft at the top of the design, adding much-needed balance. Finally, the small hot peppers were tightly strung on a durable string and tied around the central stack of husks.

Whereas the dried chili peppers serve merely as a decorative element on the harvest wreath, they form the dominant base for the kitchen wreath on page 51. The designer started with a small wire ring, which he covered with strips of raffia. He then strung several small dried peppers on a sturdy thread and wound them around the covered frame, securing both ends at the top of the ring. The point of attachment was covered with a large raffia bow, and whole cloves of garlic and a few sprigs of sage were added to the design. This kitchen wreath is as practical as it is beautiful: the cook can remove the ingredients throughout the winter for use in the kitchen and then refill the wreath in the late summer. Such decorative kitchen wreaths were common in colonial kitchens.

Top, left: This wreath was made by wrapping bundled cornhusks twice around a wire frame and securing them with strands of heavy raffia. Be sure to soak the cornhusks first and then let them dry thoroughly or the wreath will mildew. Left: Straw-based harvest wreath with raffia, Indian corn, and small hot peppers. Opposite page: Kitchen wreath with dried peppers, garlic, and sage.

© William Seitz

© Robert Hoebermann

Raffia is a long, durable fiber made from the leaves of the Madagascar palm. This material can be very easily twisted, braided, woven, and knotted, and has been used for hundreds of years for weaving baskets and mats. Raffia wreaths, easily braided from long strands of the fibrous material, are very beautiful and provide a warm, rustic look.

To make a raffia wreath, you will need a bundle of raffia strands at least 30 inches (75cm) long. (Raffia can be bought in bundles at most craft and garden stores.) Carefully pull out 2 or 3 strands of raffia from the bundle, taking care not to tangle the rest of the strands. With one of the strands, firmly tie together one end of the raffia bundle. Next, divide the loose end of the raffia bundle into 3 separate bunches for braiding. As you braid, the circular shape of the wreath is achieved by pulling the left-hand bunch a little tighter than the right one is pulled.

When you come to the end of the raffia, cross the two ends, leave a few inches extra on each, and tie them together. Wrap the knot with a loose strand of raffia to secure it well and to help the wreath retain its circular form. Once the basic wreath frame is finished, you can add dried grasses, herbs, flowers, or other basic wreath materials for decoration.

The wreath on page 52 was constructed on a braided raffia base, with garlic and sage leaves attached at bottom center and other assorted herbs and flowers tied around the wreath

with raffia strands. This combination makes for an attractive yet simple wreath. Herbal designs like this one are practical as well as pretty. Usually made when the herbs are still fresh, herbal wreaths are hung in the kitchen, and the spices are gradually removed and added as a savory blend in soups and stews.

The wreath on this page is another design utilizing a braided raffia wreath. However, instead of herbs, this wreath is embellished with a few centrally placed dried flowers and leaves.

Opposite page: Herb wreath on a raffia base, with a few dried chilies and a clove of garlic for accent. Below: Braided-raffia wreath with dried flowers and leaves set at bottom center.

© Christopher Bain

Chapter Five

Christmas
and
Holiday Wreaths

While wreaths are appropriate decorative pieces throughout the year, they take the most prominent stand during Christmastime. An evergreen wreath is a traditional Christmas decoration. In fact, when most people think of wreaths in general, they think of the evergreen wreath. The basic evergreen-wreath form can be bought premade in a variety of sizes. However, it is much more enjoyable to make your own using freshly cut greens. A homemade evergreen wreath will last much longer and will provide you with the satisfaction of having created something with your own hands.

To make such a wreath, you will need a wire wreath frame (8- or 10-inch [20 or 25cm] frames are the most functional, although any size will do), some medium-gauge green florist's wire, a pair of strong scissors or garden clippers, and a large supply of fresh evergreens cut to a uniform size. The larger the wreath frame, the longer the evergreen pieces can be. For an 8- or 10-inch (20 or 25cm) wreath, 6- to 8-inch (15 to 20cm) pieces of evergreen will suffice.

There are two basic methods for attaching the evergreens to the wire frame. One method is to simply wire each sprig to the frame, one at a time. The other method is to tie sprigs into small bundles and then attach the bundles to the wreath frame. The second method is, in my experience, the easiest and most effective way of attaching the greens. Make several clusters of 2 or 3 sprigs each by wiring them together at the base of the stems. An average wreath will use anywhere from 30 to 40 of these clusters.

Once you have a good supply of clusters ready, lay the first cluster along the top of the frame with the stems parallel to the frame and pointing to the right. Tie the end of your florist's wire to the wire frame and begin wrapping it securely around the stems

Opposite page: A beautiful basic evergreen wreath, easy to make at home, is the perfect symbol of the holiday season. Strings of red wooden beads and bright faux apples ornament this balsam wreath.

© Robert Hoebermann

© Jennifer Levy

and the frame. Make 2 or 3 wraps and then add a second cluster on the inside of the frame, again with the stems pointing to the right. Secure the second cluster with 2 or 3 wraps. Continue to add clusters of evergreens, working around the wreath in a clockwise motion and alternating from the outside to the inside of the wreath frame. When you come full circle around the wreath, gently lift the ends of the first bundle and secure the stems of the last bundle underneath. Once the wreath is completely wound, you may have to add a few clusters to help fill it out. This method is essentially the same process as winding a dried flower wreath, as described on page 11.

This basic evergreen wreath can be used in a variety of different ways to create beautiful holiday decorations. Most of the evergreen wreath bases in this chapter were made using this simple method. In the example on page 54, red wooden beads and bright faux apples and berries were added for a cheerful holiday design.

The evergreen wreaths on this page use a brass horn, which echoes the circular shape of the wreath, as an unusual decorative element. In the wreath at the top, apples were wired and tucked into clusters of blue cedar berries and ornamental pineapples. The overall feel of this wreath is one of hospitality, with a touch of festivity brought on by the gold-sprayed magnolia leaves and pinecones. The wreath underneath evokes a similar feeling, with a large bow and red tassel adding an extra flourish.

Christmas wreaths can be large or small, simple or complex. The large holiday heart wreath on this page makes use of just a few materials but arranges them in a fairly elaborate design. First, the wreath maker covered a large wire heart frame with boxwood (huckleberry or any other seasonal green would also work). The boxwood was attached by using the winding technique with green, waxed twine (see page 11). Next, crab apples were attached to florist's picks and then inserted into the greens. The wire frame and the wrapped greens provided enough support for the crab apples, so no hot glue or wire was needed. Next, a garland of popcorn, strung on simple sewing thread, was wound around the heart and secured at the top of the wreath. To hide the construction and to add a festive touch, a red satin ribbon was attached to the top of the heart.

Opposite page, top: Hospitality wreath with brass hunting horn. Opposite page, bottom: A variation on the wreath above, this design uses a brass French horn as its base, attaches evergreen branches and pinecone-and-berry clusters, then wraps the whole with a red-and-green paisley ribbon. Below: Large holiday heart wreath of boxwood, crab apples, and popcorn.

© Robert Hoebermann

Brass and evergreen are natural complements to each other. On page 58, a traditional Douglas fir wreath rings in the holiday cheer with a chain of brass sleigh bells cascading from a cluster of gold balls. Anchoring the whole design is a beautiful gold metallic ribbon and a strand of small gold beads that wraps around the entire wreath. Painted Christmas balls or gold-sprayed pinecones or seed pods could also be added to this design or used as less expensive substitutes.

In this gold-ornamented wreath, the evergreens were inserted into a tight wire base. Green nylon twine was used to secure the greens in place. Because many of the materials on this

wreath are relatively heavy, it is best to use either a wire or straw base for this wreath. Styrofoam is too fragile, and a grapevine wreath may not provide an adequate anchor for the greens.

The three-wreath display pictured on this page makes a joyous holiday door decoration. To make this display yourself, use three round evergreen wreaths of varying sizes. (The size of the wreaths will depend largely on where you will be placing them: never make the wreaths too large or too small for the space where they will hang.) This design was made with 8-, 10-, and 12-inch (20, 25, and 30cm) premade evergreen wreath frames bought at a craft store.

The designer of these wreaths generously filled out the evergreen bases with long vines of winter ivy. The ivy vines were simply wrapped around each wreath frame to the desired degree of thickness. It may be necessary to secure the vines in place with a little bit of wire; however, in most cases, the vine itself will hold the ivy to the frame. Next, sprigs of yellowed evergreen were added to provide a color contrast. A small element of surprise was then added with the clusters of green limes, attached with hot glue. You should be sure that the glue is completely dry before handling the wreaths, or else the limes will surely fall off. Lastly, the green velvet ribbon and large bow at the top were added to provide the perfect anchor for this three-wreath design.

Opposite page: Evergreen wreath wrapped with a gold chain and decorated with brass sleigh bells. Left: Boxwood, often used to make holiday roping, also makes a beautiful wreath when tightly wound around itself and secured with wire. Clusters of artificial red berries and a bow perfectly complement this wreath. Above: Triple-wreath holiday display with yellowed evergreen sprigs and limes.

The beautiful bleached-twig-and-evergreen wreath in the upper left-hand corner of this page is actually two wreaths in one. The designer started with a large wire heart for the evergreen base. He added small amounts of fresh evergreens a bit at a time and wound them securely with green waxed twine. Next, he used a smaller wire heart frame and carefully wound on the bleached twigs. The small gold and red balls and the red berries were added during the winding process to give the wreath a well-integrated look. (If you find that winding so many elements in place at the same time is too difficult, you can add the balls and berries after the twig wreath is completed.) Finally, the designer wired the two wreaths together at the tops of the two hearts, and a green ribbon and a cluster of Christmas balls were added to hide the connecting point.

The mantel is a distinguished spot for a wreath at any time of year. But at Christmas, a wreath above the fireplace is almost necessary. On page 61, a large yet simple evergreen wreath, studded with decorative pinecones, artificial berries, and a large red bow, is complemented by the placement of loose greens, red candles, and a hand-painted Santa on top of the mantel. Along with the teddy bears, the Christmas rug, the rocking horse, and the roaring fire, the whole room seems to come alive in a wonderfully heart-warming Christmas tableau.

Left: This vine wreath, filled with dried grasses, was designed for a woodland look. To complete the effect, a bird's nest was placed at the bottom with a small ceramic bird tucked into it. Above: Heart-shaped wreath with bleached twigs and evergreens. Opposite page: Traditional Christmas evergreen wreath with pinecones, artificial berries, and a large red bow.

Left: This feathery wreath is made of packing straw wrapped around a base. Fabric ribbon was tied in bows around five candy canes; then, using pale thread, these were tied at even intervals around the straw to keep everything in place. Below: Pine-needle wreath with small wooden models of houses and a village church, all wrapped with a plaid ribbon tied in a bow.

© David Arky

© David Arky

Not all Christmas wreaths have to be traditional evergreen designs. These three examples provide a welcome departure from the norm, but still convey the warmth and spirit of the holiday season. The pine-needle village wreath pictured on this page shows a creative way to alter a conventional straw base into something new and different. The designer used a basic eight-inch (20cm) straw wreath base and covered it with a layer of long pine needles. Red, Scotch, and white pine needles work best because they are long and pliable. She built a pine-needle base, carefully laying the needles against the straw ring and wrapping them with strong, thin thread. (Tan thread is the best choice because it blends in with the color of the needles.) She concentrated on small sections of the wreath at a time and gradually worked her way around. The ribbon was added for color and also to cover up some of the thread wrapping.

To attach the small wooden village figurines, the designer cut out pieces of cardboard about the same size as each house. She then glued the cardboard pieces to the wreath in the positions where she wanted the houses to ultimately lay. Next, she glued the houses to the pieces of cardboard. Using the cardboard attachments makes a strong binding between the wooden houses and the wreath. It may be necessary to secure the pieces with tape to hold them until the glue dries.

Lastly, little clusters of baby's breath were added between the houses to represent trees in the village.

The gold-painted holiday toy wreath on this page is sure to bring a smile to any child's face. A wreath similar to this one can be made from old forgotten toys that have been lying around the house or from small, inexpensive store-bought toys. Because this is a fairly heavy wreath made of awkwardly shaped objects, it is best to start with a wire wreath base. Wire bases are very sturdy and provide a solid foundation for even the most oddly shaped objects.

The designers built this wreath in three simple steps. First, they glued all of the flat-sided objects evenly around a 10-inch (25cm) wire frame. These included wood blocks, dominoes, and flat ornaments. These objects were left unpainted at this point. Next, the oddly shaped objects—cars, airplanes, apples, etc.—were lightly painted with gold spray paint. These objects need to be painted before being attached in order to cover them on all sides. Once the paint dried, they were attached securely to the wreath frame with hot glue. Take note that it may be necessary to secure some of the heavier objects with florist's wire as well. Once the glue had set, a light coat of paint was sprayed onto the entire wreath, with care taken to completely cover the unpainted objects, while not spraying the painted ones

© David Arky

too heavily. The final touch was to tie on a few gold ribbons to help fill out the open spots of the design, as well as to add a softer element to the wreath.

Holiday wreath with old or broken toys of varying size and shape, hot-glued to wire frame.

Very beautiful holiday wreaths can be made using very nontraditional materials. In fact, Christmas and New Year's are the perfect times to experiment with materials that are not normally considered the standard wreath ornaments. When one thinks of Christmas decorations, images of holly, evergreens, bright red bows, and colorful Christmas balls normally come to mind. In the unusual example on this page, the designer chose to create a festive Christmas decoration by using a combination of sea shells and pinecones. While sea shells are not normally thought of as part of Christmas—unless, perhaps you live along the seashore—they work well when combined with a collection of pinecones and dried seedpods. The shells and cones do provide natural shades of deep reds and browns, but the overall effect of this wreath depends upon its textures, and not on its colors. The scalloped lines of the shells provide a pleasant complement to the petallike quality of the cones. In addition, the thin flowing bow at the top of the wreath adds a nice focal point to the design.

The wreath on page 65 is made entirely from pinecones and seedpods. As with the previous wreath, the visual interest here comes primarily from texture as opposed to color. The varying sizes of the cones and the pods help to create a flow and rhythm to the design. The wreath maker used 6 large pinecone rosettes spaced evenly around the ring as an anchor. Between these cones he added a collection of smaller cones and pods that were placed irregularly in order to create a lot of textural contrast.

Both of the wreaths on these pages use very dense, heavy elements, which must be firmly secured to the wreath form. When using heavy materials such as these, you should be sure to choose a very sturdy wreath base. These wreaths were made by wiring *and* hot-gluing the elements to wire wreath bases. It is best to use both heavy-duty florist's wire and hot glue for wreaths of this type.

© Robert Hoebermann

Left: Unusual Christmas wreath constructed of a combination of sea shells and pinecones wired and hot-glued to a wire frame. Opposite page: Textured wire-base wreath made with pinecones and seedpods.

© Derek Fell

Above: The best place to obtain cones for your wreath is directly from the forest. Opposite page: St. Lucia's Day wreath made of boxwood, assorted leaves and flowers, and white candles.

For Swedish people, December 13 is St. Lucia's Day. At dawn on this day the eldest daughter, wearing a candle-lit head wreath called a Crown of Lights, and her female siblings go into their parents' room with a special gift of saffron bread. St. Lucia is the patron saint of eyes and vision, who bears food to restore the healthy glow of life. The saffron bread is to satisfy hunger and the candlelit wreath is to light the darkness. In addition, songs are sung to dispel the gloom of winter and to honor St. Lucia.

This St. Lucia's wreath was made by wiring boxwood onto a thin straw frame. Small tin rings were added to secure the white candles. Finally, the designers added pressed mahonia, lonicera leaves, red pepperberries, and small sprigs of Queen Anne's lace, all of which were either wired or hot-glued to the design.

The traditional St. Lucia's wreath is made with evergreens and red lingon-berries. Lingonberries, which are a relative of the cranberry, are sometimes difficult to acquire, so pepper-berries, cranberries, or holly can make adequate substitutes.

If you intend to act out the St. Lucia's tradition, be sure to wrap your daughter's head with a damp cloth to protect her hair before putting the lit wreath on her head. The St. Lucia's wreath can also be used as a table decoration or as an Advent wreath.

SOURCES

Alberta Nurseries and Seed, Ltd.
P.O. Box 20
Bowden, Alberta T0M 0K0
Canada
(plants and seeds, vegetables and flowers)

Andre Viette Farm and Nursery
Route 1, Box 16
Fishersville, Virginia
(wide selection of unusual everlastings)

Betsy Williams/The Proper Season
68 Park Street
Andover, Massachusetts 01810
(herb and dried flower wreaths)

Christian Appalachian Project
322 Crub Orchard Road
Lancaster, Kentucky 40446
(send stamped envelope for list of natural pine
and fir wreaths)

Craft Service
337 University Avenue
Rochester, New York 14607
(reed, straw, plastic, and Styrofoam wreaths)

Cramer's Posy Patch
740 High Ridge Road
Columbia, Pennsylvania 17512
(dried flowers and grapevine wreath bases)

Flag Fork Herb Farm
260 Flag Ford Road
Frankfort, Kentucky 40601
(dried flowers)

Goodwin Creek Secret Gardens
P.O. Box 83
Williams, Oregon
(plants and seeds for drying flowers)

Homestead Gardens
Pumpkin Hill Road
Warner, New Hampshire 03278
(dried flowers and grasses, cone twig, and vine
wreaths)

Lewiscraft
40 Commander Boulevard
Scarborough, Ontario
Canada M1S 3S2
(wide variety of wreaths, instructions, materials)

Sax Arts & Crafts
100A East Pleasant
Milwaukee, Wisconsin 53212
(wicking and craft supplies)

Shepherd's Garden Seeds
6116 Highway 9
Felton, California 95018
(plants and seeds for drying flowers)

INDEX